How To

Become

A

Motoring

Journalist

By

Carlton Boyce

Published by Carlton Boyce Ltd

www.carltonboyce.com

Registered office:
Geufron Hall,
Llangollen,
LL20 8DY

The Author asserts his moral right to be identified as the Author of the work in relation to all such rights as are granted by the Author to the Publisher under the terms and conditions of this Agreement.

Copyright © 2015 Carlton Boyce

All rights reserved. No part of this publication may be reproduced, distributed, or transmitted in any form or by any means, including photocopying, recording, or other electronic or mechanical methods, without the prior written permission of the publisher, except in the case of brief quotations embodied in critical reviews and certain other non-commercial uses permitted by copyright law. For permission requests, email or write to the publisher at the address shown above or via enquiries@carltonboyce.com

Disclaimer

Although the Author has made every effort to ensure that the information in this book is correct at the time of publishing, he does not assume, and hereby disclaims, any liability to any party for any loss, damage, or disruption caused by errors or omissions, whether such errors or omissions result from negligence, accident, or any other cause. If you notice an error, please contact the Author so this can be amended

Table of Contents

Introduction

Do you want it enough?

What does a motoring journalist actually do?
A typical working week
Things you might find yourself writing about
Alternative outlets for your talent
A warning

Routes into motoring journalism

Blogging
Your audience
Branding
Finding your voice
Advertorials

Automotive Journalism through Blogging

Professional associations
The Guild of Motoring Writers
Regional groups

Social media
Google+
Twitter and Facebook
YouTube
Instagram
Other channels

Killing photography, or saving it?
The technique
Seeing the world through your lens
Composition
Conclusion

Getting your inspiration
It's all about the people
Cars are boring

The two websites you must follow
Listicles
Photography - delivering the whole package
The equipment
The ten shots every art director needs
Depth of field
Shutter speed
The shortcut almost all of us take

Automotive Photography
Location, location, location
Getting the position of the car right
Choosing the best angle to shoot at
Lighting
Action shots
Processing in Photoshop

Video
Equipment
Technique

Evaluating a car
Getting hold of a car from the press fleet
Press car etiquette
Driving a car to evaluate it
Getting it all down on paper
Honing your skills
Polishing

Your first car launch
What will happen
Sharing a car
Taking notes
A warning
Post-launch

Your first race meeting or motor show
Signing on
Photographers' vests

The marshals
Get in close
Post-event

Interviewing
The three stages of every interview

The equipment you need
Computers
Phone
Camera
Laptop bag
Overnight bag

Copyright
What exactly are you selling?
What if it all goes wrong?

Pitching your work
Researching your pitch
What format to pitch in
The follow-up
One to consider
Pricing your work
Working for free
Selling it twice

Putting it all together

Don't peak too early
Hone your craft
Snaring your editor
The difficulties start here
Write the headlines first

Conclusion

7

Introduction

Every car enthusiast wants a job as a professional motoring journalist, don't they? After all, travelling the globe and getting paid to drive some of the world's finest cars while staying in five-star hotels and eating some of the best food of your life is a dream come true, isn't it?

Yes, absolutely, of course it is. And while I could bore you with tales of delayed flights, boring cars, and unpaid invoices the reality is that the life of a motoring journalist is as fantastic as you think it is and I am a very lucky man. I know that, which is why I'm going to share how I did it with you.

Five years ago I was doing a job I hated. A job I detested. I was making myself ill with stress and worry and couldn't see a way out. At the age of forty, I was too old for a career change that would pay what I was then earning and too young to retire. All I had was a dream and a love of cars. I'd written the odd short story (and one novel that was subsequently banned, but that's another story…).

So, with an arrogance born of desperation, I set myself up as a professional motoring journalist. Within six months I was earning a living; not a great one, it has to be said, but a living, nonetheless. Every year I earned more and more and I'm now at the stage where I don't have to worry about household bills anymore.

But isn't becoming a motoring journalist almost impossible, I hear you ask? After all, none other than Jeremy Clarkson, the most famous motoring journalist of us all, once pointed out that more people had been into space than are earning a full-time living writing about cars in the UK. So no, it won't be easy, but it is possible, as I've proved.

You can do it too. Just follow the steps I'm about to show you, work hard, and ride your luck and you could be driving the latest

McLaren or Ferrari around a foreign racing circuit and getting paid to do so.

Just don't forget the luck, eh?

Carlton Boyce
Llangollen
October 2015

Do you want it enough?

First, the bad news: you probably won't walk into a job as a staff writer with one of the major car magazines or websites without gaining some experience in the business first; no matter how good you are, it is highly unlikely that anyone is going to give you that opportunity sight unseen. However, the good news is that you might be able to do so in a couple of years, given the right skills and attitude.

How am I so sure? Because two colleagues have done just that by working hard and writing beautifully. They did it (and so could you, remember that!) because they did everything they could to make it happen: they blogged incessantly; they used social media to their advantage; they talked to the right people and made friends with folk throughout the automotive industry; and they worked every evening and weekend at it until they made it to the big time. They are also damned fine writers.

So the first question is: how badly do you want it? Do you want it enough to give up every evening and weekend to the keyboard for a couple of years? Enough to finance your own road trips to write about? Enough to pay for photographic and driving courses to build your skillset? Enough to gain the necessary writing skills to be able to twist the English language to your own ends?

If the answer the every question is a resounding 'hell yes!' then you will be able to make your dream come true; it isn't impossible but it is hard work.

Let's make a start, shall we?

What does a motoring journalist actually do?

The life of a motoring journalist is hugely varied, which is part of the appeal for most of us. Some days are spent sitting behind a computer, churning out word after word for hour after hour to a backbeat of Springsteen and coffee. (The Springsteen is optional, the coffee isn't.) Others are spent driving fast cars in beautiful locations for mile after mile with your only concern being whether today's lunch will be as good as last night's dinner.

You'll also spend more of your life waiting in a departure lounge than seems possible. Chasing overdue invoices isn't much fun either and pitching new features strikes fear into even the stoutest motoring journalist's heart. Interviews with bank managers who want to talk about overdrafts rank pretty low on my list of ways to spend an hour too.

Like I said, it's a varied job.

A typical working week

A typical working week for me, if there is such a thing, might look something like this:

Monday I'm up early to get to Manchester airport to catch an eight o'clock flight to Germany. This means getting up at four and creeping out of the house *sans* coffee before trying to start this week's press car quietly. It's a Jaguar F-TYPE, a car that doesn't understand the meaning of discretion, so my departure is marked by a six-cylinder bark. I suppose I should feel guilty but it did sound nice. I arrive in Germany and then spend three hours in a minibus before arriving at a multi-lingual press conference. Then lunch, before I finally get to drive a new commercial van around the Bosch test track. Then back to the hotel for a shower and pre-dinner drinks before sitting down to eat at eight. I can't drink too much as I'm driving the next day.

Tuesday brings a relatively leisurely breakfast before another three hours in a minibus returning to the airport. Check-in, sit around, discover the flight has been delayed and drink too much coffee. Arrive back in the UK three hours late, which gives me time to drive home, scoff some dinner and catch up with the family before bed.

Wednesday is press car changeover day, which is fine as I'm stuck behind the computer all day writing. A last drive in the F-TYPE to the train station to collect the Jaguar driver reminds me what a lovely thing it is, both to look at and to drive. Then a SEAT Mii turns up in a cheery yellow. It's one of my favourite small cars so it's no trouble to pop the chap who delivered it to the same train station I collected Jaguar man from. More writing and then an early finish at four o'clock.

Thursday means more travelling, this time to a UK launch in The Cotswolds (aren't they all?). I'm not in any hurry, so I meander along the Welsh Marches in lieu of the motorway. The little Mii is terrific fun, not fast but very willing and there's real fun to be had in a slow car that you can drive flat-out for mile after mile. Arrive at the hotel to find a piece I sent off yesterday needs a few alterations so I do these in the lull between arriving and eating, missing out on the pre-dinner drinks.

Friday is all about driving a 'new' car that is nothing of the sort: new front and rear bumpers, some trim changes, and a new engine do not a new car make. I leave after lunch, winding my way back along the Marches in the Mii and am home in time for supper.

Saturday is spent writing up yesterday's launch plus tidying off a piece I started last week. It's a buyers' guide for a classic car, something I love doing and an area of work that pays much better than writing about new metal. (I'm so impressed by the car I'm researching and writing about that I later buy one. This is one of the many perils of writing about old cars.)

Sunday is a quieter day. I wash the Mii and take it out for a drive and to photograph it. Most outlets are happy with the manufacturer's stock images but it's good to have a bank of your own work to draw against when the need arises. Besides, I'm driving a fun car in the beautiful Welsh countryside, stopping in fabulous locations to shoot it. It's not exactly demanding work, is it?

Things you might find yourself writing about

Writing about new cars is what everyone thinks of when they imagine the life of a motoring journalist. It's also the gig everyone wants, which depresses the price you'll get paid for it. There's no denying that it's fun, it's just hard to pay the bills if that's all you do. So how does a freelance motoring writer earn a living wage?

Well, you can write about stuff other than new cars. Consumer guides pay quite well, so brush up on the action to take after you've had an accident, or work on a piece that describes what the seven changes to company car taxation that have just been announced will mean to the average company car driver. Buyers' guides are good fun to write and tend to pay reasonably. However, the research can take a long time, making the pay-per-hour less impressive than the top-line figure might have you believe. This is less of a problem if you keep all your working notes and sell a similar piece to someone else in the future.

Selling photographs pays well once you've got your head around the subject, so it's worth joining a few online websites and uploading your work there. Rates vary but £50-ish per image isn't to be sniffed at and it provides a steady, if low, stream of income to supplement the other stuff you do. I also shoot to commission, which doesn't happen very often but pays very well when it does: £250-500 per image is good work and stock image photography can pay very well indeed if you can get your head around the pictures that sell and are prepared to put in the hours shooting hundreds of images.

Alternative outlets for your talent

As journalists and writers we prostitute ourselves more than the public might imagine. Some find themselves crossing the divide onto the Dark Side and working for the very PRs we are supposed to be keeping at arm's length by writing press releases for various car manufacturers.

Others might find themselves working out a driving route for the launch of a new model before going on to draw up the tulip diagrams that we all hate so much when we get lost.

I once spent a couple of years working part-time launching a car manufacturer's social media platform before going on to act as its community manager and content creator, a gig that was great fun and paid me very well indeed. In fact, the whole social media arena remains an untapped source and is well worth exploring as an alternative funding stream. As one senior executive in the automotive industry who was charged with launching his company's global social media strategy told me: "We know nothing about it. Absolutely nothing. We're just throwing money at it because we're scared of what might happen if we don't."

What I trying to say in my usual bumbling fashion is that you have three skills that are in high demand: a vivid imagination; the ability to write fluently and elegantly; and a talent for producing compelling images. These are talents that people will pay well for, you just have to use that imagination to find those willing to pay you for them.

A warning

You will prostitute yourself because if you don't, you'll starve and be forced to go back into the real world and wear a tie again. So you will do it but that doesn't mean you are selling your integrity, just your skills.

So when you write an advertorial, you must tell everyone that it's a sponsored piece. Yes, Google hates it and will penalize you for it and the PR people will beg you not to tell anyone but you must because your integrity is worth more than they could possibly pay you.

The same goers for free press junkets. We all have our own moral compass and mine draws the line at a week's skiing or spending the day watching football in a sponsor's hospitality box as the guest of a car manufacturer. Others feel differently and I'm not here to be critical of anyone else's judgments and decisions, I'm just here to tell you that it happens so you're prepared when you receive the emailed invitation.

Simply put, if it is directly or even indirectly connected with what I'm being paid for I see no harm in accepting hospitality from a car manufacturer. If it is completely disassociated then I'm out. You'll make your own mind up but just don't blithely accept because you think everyone else does it because we don't.

Summary

- It's not all about driving new cars.
- Consumer advice pays well.
- Don't prostitute yourself too cheaply.
- Freebies are never free.

Routes into motoring journalism

Don't get me wrong; accurately evaluating a car's dynamic behaviour around the *evo* Triangle in North Wales might be a core skill (and a whole lot of fun) but it probably isn't the most important one if you are to fulfil your dream of becoming a professional motoring writer because every successful motoring journalist from Jeremy Clarkson to LJK Setright is, primarily, a skilful writer that just happens to write about cars.

That's an important distinction to note and it's good news for you because while there are an awful lot of good drivers out there, few of them are able to express themselves in a way that engages the reader, which means there is plenty of demand for new talent.

So the demand is there and it is, for the most part, unfilled. An editor of a well-known motoring magazine commented recently that it is hard to find graduates who can spell accurately, much less write well.

One of the more obvious routes might be to study for a post-graduate degree in Automotive Journalism at Coventry University – but even the tutors there would accept there are many paths into the profession, few of which require formal qualifications. If you do decide to enrol then you are wise beyond your years but don't expect the course to offer any short cuts into the industry, just a solid grounding in the basics of the job...

If there is a short cut (and I remain unconvinced that such a thing exists) then it might the Sir William Lyons Award, run every year by the Guild of Motoring Writers. Open to aspiring writers aged 17-23, it offers a first prize of £2,000 and lots of publicity. Previous winners have generally done very well but competition is fierce and it is aimed at the younger journalist rather than someone who is changing careers in their middle years as I did.

So if we rule out formal study, and shortcuts via awards, we are left with what has rapidly become the *de facto* way of joining the industry: blogging.

Summary

- There are no shortcuts into motoring journalism.
- Your ability to spell and write grammatically will be far more helpful than your ability to drift.
- Start a blog.

Blogging

It was almost impossible to break into motoring journalism before the advent of blogging; now anyone can call himself or herself a motoring journalist once they've published a motoring blog. This is, you might argue, a bad thing but it is democratic journalism in practice: if you write well people will read you and if you don't, they won't. And that is, after all, the only thing that really matters.

Your audience

Never forget the audience you are writing for; get that wrong and you've stalled before you even started. So please try to remember that you are not writing to impress anyone; you are writing to provide someone, somewhere, with a damned good read and if you don't get that bit right they'll turn the page without a second thought.

So write with your audience in mind, and keep it simple. LJK Setright was famously verbose, frequently resorting to Latin to make a point. Do not try and write like that because you are not, and never will be, him. Nor are you Jeremy Clarkson, so go easy on the metaphors and similes.

Keep your sentences short and write in neat paragraphs. Make it easy for your reader to keep track of what you're saying, and why. Explain things in simple terms and never assume their knowledge is as wide-ranging as yours. But then never patronize them either.

Branding

Getting the name of your blog right is essential: you need something that's evocative, unique, and catchy. Once you've thought of something good you need to check that the name is also free on Twitter, Facebook, Instagram, YouTube, and Google+. This is harder than it sounds but it's essential to get your brand's marketing consistent.

Brand? Yes, your brand and every brand needs a logo so pay someone to design one. There are thousands of people out there that will design one for under £20, so don't be a cheapskate and do it yourself unless you are a graphic designer. Once you're happy with the logo, use it in your email signature, across your social media platforms, and at the top of your website.

Finding your voice

Now write often and find your own voice. Too many writers (me included) write in the same formulaic way. If you can, get hold of a few copies of *CAR* magazine from the late 1970s and 1980s and read Russell Bulgin, Phil Llewellin, and George Bishop. All of them could tell a story that had nothing whatsoever to do with the way a car was engineered or how it drove. By contrast, LJK Setright was a master at describing a car's engineering and was, despite being impenetrable at times, a compelling writer who generated as much light as heat.

Other notable writers include Alan Clark and P.J. O'Rourke, neither of whom are motoring journalists in the purest sense but both of whom write beautifully about cars.

Don't ignore Jeremy Clarkson either. Like him or loathe him, there is no denying that he is extraordinarily talented, writing prolifically and churning out some of the highest quality pieces you'll ever read. His book *I Know You Got Soul* stands as one of the most eloquent and haunting books you'll ever read – and that he's writing about a subject as potentially dry as engineering makes his fluency even more impressive.

In fact, most of the motoring journalists who write for the weekend papers are brilliant at producing interesting articles about cars that are, sometimes, no better than mundane.

All of these writers found their own voice, their own way of approaching a car, their own priorities and all of them were able to write on any subject and make it interesting. It isn't easy but try to find your own way of making the incomprehensive compelling, and the dry warm and witty. If you do you'll never be short of work.

Advertorials

If you produce anything that is even half-decent someone will approach you, asking you to publish an advertorial on your blog. You should be very careful before you agree, even if the money (typically between £25 and £150) seems attractive.

Advertorials – where an advert is disguised as an editorial piece – are almost always half-baked and poorly written (I've never, ever received one that is even that well written, but heh, I'm here to spread the love, not hate...) and won't fool anyone into thinking they're anything other than a paid advert.

I have published them but I have always insisted on making it very clear that it is an advertorial or sponsored post. This irritates the sponsor, who doesn't want it to look like an advert. Nonetheless, they will sometimes agree to your terms, which make it almost acceptable in my view.

If you publish an advertorial without declaring it you will lose credibility on a massive scale and may face Google sanctions if anyone else has published the same thing elsewhere. (Google may punish you if you declare it as a sponsored post anyway, but that's a different matter.)

Having said all this, writing the advertorials for someone else to publish is a completely different thing. It doesn't pay much but then it doesn't take long either - and no one will know you've written it anyway.

Summary

- Your blog is your marketplace - and it can be your source of shiny new cars and exotic car launch invitations.
- Your blog is where you will find your voice and develop your style and is a place where you can be you. (To a certain extent, at least.)
- Beware of advertorials.
- Read the masters but don't copy them. That would be ridiculous.

Automotive Journalism through Blogging
by Adam Tudor-Lane

Adam Tudor-Lane started his career as a motoring writer by writing in his spare time for the Peugeot owners' club. After plugging away for a while he was invited to the launch of the Peugeot 208 in June 2012 where he found himself sharing a car with me.

He started blogging more widely in the same year, covering brands and manufacturers other than Peugeot with a professionalism that is rare and I've watched his meteoric rise with more than the usual interest.

How has he turned carwitter *(*http://carwitter.com/*) into one of the most popular motoring websites in the UK in under three years? Well, it's the usual triumvirate of hard work, professionalism, and talent. Here is the man himself explaining what he did, how and why:*

Becoming a "professional" automotive journalist (if there is such a thing) is a very closed shop. Unless you have studied some form of journalism at a university, then committed to the rounds of unpaid work experience with numerous magazines, you pretty much have no hope of breaking into the industry – and even if you do follow these steps, it is still ludicrously hard to gain a full-time position with a large outlet.

So I did what many are now doing and started writing my own blog.

After meeting Carlton at a car launch (that I was lucky enough to blag an invitation for) three years ago, I pestered him for a full 24 hours, trying to learn as much about automotive journalism as I could. After his encouragement, I decided to set up my own website a month or so later.

But I wanted it to be professional, not like some of the over-personal, self-blown-trumpet affairs. It had to be as good as the big boys, because if it wasn't, there was no point in doing it.

Coming up with a name was the hardest part. It had to stand out, be different and, most importantly, have the .co.uk and .com domain names available. While thinking up all manner of great names I soon realised that most of them had already been taken, so I resulted to typing random musings directly into a domain host to check the availability before I got too attached.

After a few days I had come up with one where both the domain names and the social media (except Twitter - annoyingly) were free and ready to use. I wasn't overly keen on the name, but it had a sort of ring to it and was easy to remember, largely due to the borrowed second half – *Carwitter* was born.

Having a little web knowledge I installed Wordpress without too many problems, found a fairly decent theme template, and went about fudging together some HTML and CSS changes to make it more personalised. I asked a good friend to come up with a few logo designs around a rough brief, and after a week or so settled on a small, speeding bubble car and some twitter-esque writing. Now I had a brand.

The plan was to write the occasional car review, maybe a few words about any motoring events I attended, and that was about it. But after securing my first press cars from a very generous manufacturer I soon realised I couldn't just put out one review a month because nobody would ever visit the website!

I realised that I had to cover the news too. So selecting the stories I felt were interesting, and breaking them down into bite size chunks with just the facts, the website soon had a healthy amount of content.

My writing skills were developing daily, in fact they are still developing to this day, ever improving in my own mind but never being quite sure of how good my words are - after all I'm just a lowly "blogger".

And bloggers get a very bad name amongst the so-called "professional" auto journalists. Apparently, we work for free, stealing non-existent money straight out of their bank accounts, making blogging a dirty word, frowned upon, even.

But without blogging how can mere mortals - from their mid-twenties onwards - gain any real experience in this field? I certainly couldn't take a month out of my normal 9-5 job to go and work as an intern at one of the big magazines; I have a house, bills, and car loans to pay for. It seems to me that automotive journalism is very much this niche club, with the majority already in it being there from the olden days when printed press ruled the roost and paid jobs were plentiful, but since the invention of the Internet nobody has really caught up with the times. New media is the root of all evil they say, especially me and my blog. I am made to feel that I am single handedly killing the industry I'm trying to break into.

I may not have ever studied journalism; I may not have a degree from Coventry's wonderful Automotive Journalism course; but what I do have is a fairly decent grasp of the English language and a passion for cars. Surely this makes me as good as anyone else?

Back to Carwitter though. I'm a big believer that if you are going to do something, you do it right. You have to commit fully and put the effort in and reviewing a car is the same for me.

So when a car manufacturer delivers a car to my door, with a tank full of fuel, and says "I will see you in a week" that means a hell of a lot to me. I don't see it as my God-given right; it's a bloody privilege, which is why I think the least I can do is take my own imagery of every single car I review.

I cannot stand press shots. Over-edited and over-used by every single media outlet that has ever written about that car. The big boys take their own pictures, so I take my own pictures. To make sure everyone knows this (and so that they aren't stolen by others and used across the Internet) I had bespoke *Carwitter* number plates made up. These are used on every shoot and have even journeyed to Europe with me.

My usual routine is to get up early on a Saturday morning, load up the car with some basic cleaning equipment, my camera gear and drive out to find a location for the photoshoot. For me the ritual of a photoshoot is a big thing, I love doing it, you get to spend a good hour or two seeing the car in a different way. Catching some new angles or noticing things that would otherwise go overlooked, and if I have picked out a particular feature in my review I can back that up with a precise image.

The way I see it is that the manufacturer has invested a lot in me by loaning me the vehicle, so the very least I can do is be bothered to take some cracking shots for them too.

I started out with a Samsung point-and-shoot camera in the early days but soon realised that however good those images were I could improve on them. So I invested and purchased an entry level Sony DSLR. I couldn't afford to lay down that amount in full so I paid it off on interest-free credit over the coming year. But the quality of the shots I can now get with it is spot-on.

And why do I get up early on a Saturday to shoot the cars? Well, if it's raining, or I'm not quite happy with the pictures, I can go out again on Sunday morning before I go back to the 9-5 job on Monday.

The first 8 months or so was a slow but steady start for *Carwitter*. I came in from work and spent a good 2 to 3 hours each evening combing through the news, often writing 4 or 5 articles ready for posting online the next day. I managed to secure some driving event invitations and started to build relationships with the industry's PR's.

But I soon realised that *Carwitter* wouldn't ever make any serious money, but then this was never the aim when I started out. However, I started to realise that *Carwitter* could be used as a platform for others like myself: a shop window for their writing; a way to gain experience in the industry; to help launch others as automotive journalists; or simply as an outlet for a shared passion.

So I decided that I would open the doors and invite others to contribute to the site. I offered nothing in return but a steadily growing window that seemed to be garnering a little bit of attention here and there.

After a few months and many emails I had a team of regular writers. Two of them were purely passionate about motorsport, so just wanted to cover race meets and have a good time along the way, but the other two saw the potential in using it as a springboard for their talents and careers.

One covered the news religiously for the site, outing articles before I even spotted they had broken. After a year of this he applied for his first job in the auto journo world (at the Goodwood Road & Racing Club, no less), and got it.

The other is a tad younger and still at university but since reading his first email many years ago I can tell he is destined for great things. He will no doubt have a place at one of the major outlets in a few years time!

Others on the site, including myself, have garnered many freelance contracts from having our words on *Carwitter*. So yes, we are putting out content for free, but those experiences and those reviews are earning money in print and on the web elsewhere.

As the team grew and we started attending events, it was time we made our presence known. I had lanyards made up, t-shirts created, and even metal ID tags with the sites details on. The professional look and feel are what make the brand, along with one other thing - consistency.

Many blogs appear and vanish all too quickly, and a fair few have since *carwitter*'s inception and that isn't a good thing. How are press offices meant to trust newer sites, if they think they are just going to rape and pillage the press fleet for a year before evaporating?

For me it has to be consistently good content, on a regular basis. It may not be up to the standards of *evo* or *Autocar* but it is as close as I can make it with a near-zero budget.

Three years in and I am amazed at how much the website has grown. We are now regularly invited to attend international launches and I turn down far more than I can actually make because of the dreaded 9-5.

We are also able to command press cars from the likes of Porsche, Jaguar, and Rolls Royce, and the defining moment came for me roughly a year ago when I attended a launch in Spain.

A well-regarded journalist once asked me what website I was from. I told him and he said that he had heard of it and visited us numerous times. He then said: "So, who owns you guys?" That line right there made me smile. Lots.

All photos in this chapter are © carwitter

Professional associations

There are a number of professional associations you could join, but probably only two that are worth joining. One is the nearest thing we've got to a professional body for the industry, the Guild of Motoring Writers. The other is your regional motoring writers' group.

The Guild of Motoring Writers

The Guild of Motoring Writers (http://www.gomw.co.uk/) was formed in 1944 and remains the largest organization of professional motoring writers, editors, broadcasters, and photographers in the world.

Two levels of membership are available: full, for those who earn a living doing nothing but writing, photographing and talking about cars; and associate membership, for those starting out in their career who might have a 'proper' job initially or have less experience.

The criteria for membership is rigorous but not onerous, and the membership fee is easily recouped by using the many benefits available to members. More importantly, it provides a level of credibility that's hard to gain elsewhere. You should join, or work towards gaining the experience to make you eligible.

Regional groups

The second option is to join your local regional motoring writers' group. Membership criteria and subscriptions will vary, so you'll need to contact them and ask.

Being a member of a regional group brings its own benefits, including exclusive manufacturer test days and weekends and invitations to new model launches.

Contact details for each group are here:

Western Group of Motoring Writers –
http://www.thewesterngroup.co.uk/

Midland Group of Motoring Writers – http://www.mgmw.org.uk/

Southern Group of Motoring Writers - http://www.sgmw.org.uk/

Northern Group of Motoring Writers – http://www.ngmw.co.uk/

Welsh Motoring Writers – http://www.motoringwriters.com/

North of Scotland Motoring Writers – http://www.nsmw.co.uk/

Ulster Motoring Writers Association - tel: 02890783220

Social media

When I started out social media was just getting into its stride, although few knew that back then. I was lucky and snagged @motoringjourno on Twitter and @motoring_journo on Instagram, the two platforms that work best for me. (I'm on Facebook, Google+ and YouTube too, but they matter much less in terms of branding for me, although they might – should? – be more important to you.)

Social media is a crowded place now, so you'll need to be a bit more creative with your name than I was, which is no bad thing; if I was starting again I might not have been so lazy as to chose such an obvious name.

Google+

Google+ is only important for Google ranking and even that is changing. So, have a presence but just cut'n'paste your Facebook stuff. No one will read it, no one will care about it, but Google will crawl all over it and rank you accordingly. Need I say more?

Twitter and Facebook

Twitter is traditionally seen as less important than Facebook in terms of social media engagement but my experience in journalism is that this isn't the case, especially when it comes to forging relationships and interacting with other writers.

So while Twitter is a no-brainer, try and define what you want to get from it before you start tweeting. Outline, even in your own mind, how you'll know you've achieved what you want to achieve: is it the total number of followers, or engagement with others, or brand definition?

Once you're up-and-running you need to start following people. Motoring journalists are a good place to start - although you'll have to resist a tendency to feel jealous when you see they're on a launch you weren't invited to – as are the manufacturers. You'll quickly develop a network of voices you like and trust and @AutoTweetUp meets are a great place to put a face to a Twitter name.

Identify the key influencers in your field and monitor them at least once a day. Engage with them, tag them, RT them; anything to get them to follow and RT you. Respond to everyone, no matter how awkward or downright weird they are. And never be defensive. Engage them, talk to them and make them feel like you care. They will engage in a positive way.

Now ask yourself why someone should follow you. Can you give them exclusive information or behind-the-scenes access, for example? Others will love to live vicariously through you: you are living the dream, after all!

Have an opinion. It should consistent with your brand image and identity but it is OK to polarize opinion – as long as it isn't offensive. Define your voice. The best voice will generally be your own...

You don't have to be the first to share something, but you do have to do it in a way that captures people's attention: topicality is more important than speed and strong images create engagement.

Monitor when your posts engender maximum engagement. This will usually be in the evenings and lunchtimes/evenings at the weekends but your feed might differ.

YouTube

The importance of video for a motoring journalist cannot be over-estimated. Many, especially those under 25, reject traditional media such as television, newspapers and magazines in favour of on-demand services like YouTube. For many being restricted to a pre-formulated programme at set times is anathema and a restrictive regimen that the Internet bypasses seamlessly.

It's hard to make a living through YouTube though, no matter what you might hear. Chris Harris, probably the most commercially successful motoring journalist working outside of *Top Gear,* claimed in July 2014 that his video of the McLaren P1 had in excess of 3.6 million views but generated only £9,200 in advertising revenue.

But despite the fact that it won't generate you a living by itself – a common theme in the world you're about to enter – you do need video. But it doesn't have to be big, expensive video recorded in 4K with Dolby sound and weeks in the making because your iPhone will do a decent job, at a pinch and if you have a DSLR you can create broadcast-quality productions using almost the same equipment as you use to take stills.

The chapter on video will tell you how.

Instagram

This is where your iPhone or Smartphone will reap dividends. Take a quick shot of your car, fiddle with it in Snapseed or similar, and post it with a few hashtags. *Voila!*

It's probably more complicated than that, so let me introduce you to Andrew Green in the next chapter, one of the most innovative photographers out there and a genius with an iPhone and simple editing apps. I first came across Andrew when I was running McLaren Automotive's social media platforms and he entered a competition we were running. He blew me away with his composition and keen eye for a great photograph and he ended up covering the launch of a Formula One car for us. Please turn to the next chapter to read what he's got to say on shooting with just a phone for social media.

Other channels

Periscope, a video-streaming app, was designed to be "the closest thing to teleportation". A bold claim but it let you see the world through the perspective of another person in real-time. I've never used it but it has a good – and growing – following, so you might like to include its use in car reviews, product launches, motor shows and the like.

Pinterest is an online collect of stuff you find interesting. You 'pin' it to one of a number of online boards (hence 'Pinterest') you've created, sharing it with others. It's an interesting idea and one I religiously compiled for a couple of years but in the end inertia and the lack of a tangible benefit led to slippage that led inexorably to abandonment. It is good for building ranking on Google, apparently.

Flickr is an online photo sharing and filing platform. I've never used it but a lot of my photographer colleagues have.

LinkedIn is supposed to be a business-networking tool. Again, I used it religiously for years and found no discernable benefit at all. I don't use it now.

Finally, Vimeo. Professionals love it for its more serious content, clean layout and lack of advertisements. YouTube will get you more viewers. Only you know what's more important to you and your developing business.

Summary

- Social media is all about building, and nurturing, relationships. It's not date rape.
- If you haven't got anything nice to say on social media, don't say anything. You might think you're being edgy and snarky but others will probably just think you're being a dick.
- If you have a press car or are at the launch of a new car or at a manufacturer's test day then tweet about it. Post photos on Instagram and tag everyone involved. Use hashtags wisely (lots on Instagram but no more than two on Twitter and Facebook and don't, no matter what, use the ones the car manufacturer 'suggests' you use) to let people find what you have posted. Retweets and likes gain you followers and credibility.

Killing photography, or saving it?
by Andrew Green

Camera phones; love them or loathe them: they're either killing photography or proving the adage that the best camera is the one you have with you. This is a debate I see raging on Internet forums all the time and I'm firmly in – both camps.

Advances in camera phone technology continue at such a pace that there is really is no reason why camera phones can't take high quality photographs that can – on social media, at least – rival those taken with a DSLR. (Well, that's not quite true. There is a reason why not, but that applies to any form of camera all the way back to the inception of photography, and that reason is the user!)

The extremes I see of this are giant-sized photos on the sides of buildings shot as part of the 'Shot on iPhone' campaign which demonstrate just how good the results can be all the way down to the millions of pictures of cats or people's dinner on Instagram that are either too dark or too bright, (unintentionally) out of focus, and poorly composed as the photographer hasn't given it a second's thought.

This why I understand why some argue that phone photography is killing photography because there are now millions, if not billions, of truly terrible photographs out there that would not have been there before

But it doesn't have to be this way and the advantages of iPhone photography and Instagram far outweigh these because millions of great photographs are now being taken that would not have been before - and Instagram is a brilliant showcase that not only allows you to show off your own work but to be inspired and to learn from others.

The technique

The fundamentals of phone photography are the same as any other: you put something interesting in front of the lens, then consider light, composition and framing. Get those right and you're more than halfway there.

The limitations of the camera on your phone are that it isn't as good in low light as even a cheap digital camera and that it probably has a much-reduced zoom (if indeed, it has a zoom). But these limitations can be seen as a challenge and using a phone to shoot sharpens you as a photographer, making you work harder, reducing complacency.

When you are first starting out you need to consider whether to use an app to shoot with or whether you are going to be traditional and just use the camera as it is. You then need to decide whether you are going to be applying filters and post-production techniques to the image to enhance the final result. There is no right or wrong way to do this but no filter is going to turn a bad photograph into a good one.

Seeing the world through your lens

For me, photography means walking round with your eyes open and looking and seeing things as you go about your daily life. Most people walk blindly from point A to point B, while photographers look around at their environment and see things in a different way. (Admittedly photographers' journeys probably take twice as long as other people as a result, but that's by the by!)

When I am walking round I look out for colours, for textures, for interesting shapes, and for things in unusual places that you wouldn't expect to see them. For interesting people with interesting outfits. But interesting doesn't have to mean beautiful, it can be young, old, new, bright, shiny, weather-beaten or decaying.

Composition

When you have your subject, always think about is the final result: is it going to be portrait, landscape or square format? Will the final image be in colour or black and white? And where do I intend to put up my finished work?

It's now that the traditional parts of photography apply. You have your subject, now use your feet to get the best angles to create an interesting composition. Don't be afraid to kneel down or lie down to get the best shot because shooting from eye-level gives you a picture taken from an angle we see everyday.

Shooting cars is much the same. For instance, a straight-on shot of a car isn't necessarily the most interesting angle to shoot from, so look to see its design features, interesting angles and curves. Be bold and go abstract and fill the frame with individual parts of the car.

Your subject doesn't have to centered: the Rule of Thirds can be used here just as you would do with more conventional forms of photography. Using leading lines to draw your viewer in, use silhouettes and shadow and concentrate on creating interest.

Always, always consider light, because it is fundamental to all photography. I find it useful to look at faces, for example, with the naked eye away from the camera first to see how the light falls upon the subject before positioning them or me to achieve the affect I want.

While doing this, take into consideration the background too. Try to get something in there that complements the foreground yet doesn't distract from the main focus of your picture. Again, don't be afraid to move yourself or your subject (if possible) to get the best combination of light, subject foreground, and background

Conclusion

A photograph is a combination of many elements and works best when they are all are brought together to complement each other.

Using your phone to bring them together needs as much time and effort as it would if you were using a DSLR or any other digital camera. You have to put the emphasis on quality over quantity, to consider each shot before you take it, and then review what you have done before adjusting accordingly.
Most of all have fun with it. Photography will open your eyes to see

all that surrounds you, and there is so much to see!

Andrew Green at agphotography@live.co.uk

All photos in this chapter are © Andrew Green

Getting your inspiration

The hardest thing about writing for a living is thinking up an angle, a pitch, and a story. It's got to be eye-catching, unique and deliverable. It's also got to be cost-effective (this is a going to be a profession, not a hobby, right?), which will rule out at least half of what you want to do.

So you need to be flexible, innovative and enquiring. As an example, my first paid piece came about because of an embarrassing fail-to-proceed during a hillclimb school at Harewood in Yorkshire. My Porsche 911 was suffering from an intermittent ignition fault and decided that midway up Harewood Hill would be the ideal time to expire. My backup car was an old Range Rover Classic, which was slow but still great fun – and fun always makes for a great story. So I contacted a car magazine and asked the editor if he'd be interested in a story about hillclimbing a Range Rover. He snapped my hand off, sending a professional photographer up from Peterborough (you'll quickly learn that most car magazines are based in Peterborough…) to recreate the day. I got paid but after six months he decided he didn't want to publish the story after all, which worked out well because I sold it again to Practical Classics magazine.

Another example is the pedal car museum I visited in France. I thought it was fascinating and realised that if I did, others would too, which meant that someone, somewhere, would pay for it. So I took photos and notes and pitched the story, selling it quickly to Classic and Sports Car magazine. And so my career began…

Driver
RESTORE IT, DRIVE IT!

At home in the Range

**Huge car, tiny curves, steep hill…
Can a Range Rover Classic handle a hillclimb?
Carlton Boyce finds out**

PHOTOS: GRAEME DUNCOMBE

PLODDING through the racing line.

A GREAT DANE among whippets.

'FASTER RANGEY, FASTER'
It might not be the quickest at the hillclimb but when it comes to fun the Range Rover is up there with the best of them.

The Range Rover Classic was designed for many things – but not tarmac track hillclimbing. Too long, too big, too cumbersome, too high. All this, however, is of no consequence, because using it for hillclimbing is magnificent fun.

For a start there's hardly any body-roll, even on that last, desperate, throw-it-across-the-line bend – and that's down to the air suspension. In addition, the V8, with the auto box locked into second gear, is a willing engine with heaps of low down torque. Also, the steering is pretty precise and the high driving position ▶

To subscribe to PC go to www.greatmagazines.co.uk

PRACTICAL CLASSICS // OCTOBER 2011 **31**

It's all about the people

The second mistake you'll make is to assume that you're writing about cars. You aren't, you are writing about the people. People make a story, while cars provide the context.

So when I went to Northern Ireland for four days as a guest of the tourist board to celebrate the 50th anniversary of Paddy Hopkirk's Monte Carlo Rally win, the subsequent story was about Paddy and Northern Ireland rather than the beautifully recreated replica of his winning Mini; the car was fabulous, but Paddy was fascinating.

And the people of Northern Ireland were even more so; for someone who grew up in The Troubles, Belfast wasn't at all what I was expecting…

© Andrew Green

The McLaren F1, still the fastest naturally aspirated car in the world and in the fantasy garage of most car enthusiasts, happens to have the best owners' handbook I've ever seen, but it's a book, albeit a beautiful one.

However, the guy who designed it and drew the artwork is a fascinating character and played a central role in the subsequent article in Octane magazine.

I could go on, but hopefully you are getting the picture: it's about the people, never the car.

Josh Clason at Depth of Speed (http://vimeo.com/24882005) is a filmatic genius and is especially adept at finding the human angle, providing inspiration to videographers, writers and photographers alike.

Cars are boring

It might seem an odd thing for me to write, given that cars are how I earn my living but it's true: cars are boring, it's what we do with them that makes them interesting. So, unless you are writing a brief news story about the release of a new model, you need to put the car into context and telling a story is the easiest way to do that.

So when you write about your own car (and why wouldn't you? It's the easiest way to get your hands on something to write about), try and find a way to put it into a story rather than making it the story.

Let me explain.

Lets assume you own a run-of-the-mill, rather dull, hatchback. You could write about going shopping in it, or driving to the coast, or even taking it on a track-day and thrashing the bejesus out of it. Who knows, if you are more talented than me (not hard...), it might even make a decent story.

But it would be much easier to write a great story by taking it out of its comfort zone and doing something interesting with it. Like driving it around the whole of the United Kingdom under the banner *Banger does Britain* (http://petroleumvitae.com/category/banger-does-britain/).

This is exactly what blogger Keith W.R. Jones did with a Rover 620 and wrote a series of pieces on the journey that helped him gain the Breakthrough Blogger award in 2012 from the Guild of Motoring Writers. Keith now writes for a major UK motoring magazine and website and freelances for a number of other outlets including CAR magazine and national newspapers.

The two websites you must follow

You should have these two websites open constantly as they'll be providing the lifeblood of your writing day. The first is Newspress (http://www.newspress.co.uk/), probably the most widely read of them all and the one most of us go to first. It will provide you with news stories, press releases, images and video footage of new cars, pretty much all of which will be available to use in your stories without charge.

The second is that of the SMMT or Society of Motor Manufacturers and Traders (http://www.smmt.co.uk/). It's a great source of facts and figures and will often give you ideas on what to write about – how is, of course, what sets you apart from the rest!

You should also register on every car manufacturer's media website. It's free of charge and you'll have no trouble being accepted as long as you've got a blog. Which you will have, if you've followed the advice I gave earlier in the book.

Listicles

Some people see listicles – lists disguised as articles – as the work of the devil. Others worry that writing them will stop them being seen as 'serious' writers, whatever that means.

I love them. They're a rich source of income and there are an almost endless number of subjects you can use for inspiration. Luckily for me, everyone else loves them too: think of an outlet, no matter how serious, and they will have published listicles.

So you need to write listicles and you need to get it right; the fact that some people don't like them is no excuse for sloppy writing.

The trick is to give the editor something they can't find anywhere else. So when you write an article on The Ten Things You Can Do To

Prepare Your Car For Winter (and you will, trust me on that) you can do what the rest of us do and write it in four stages:

1. Write down the things that spring to mind instantly.
2. Google the subject and see what everyone else has written and steal some of their ideas. Use forums, blogs, and professional websites that cover the area you are writing about too.
3. Now find the photographs to go with it. This is where a well-stocked image library of your own pays dividends.
4. Finally, spend an hour trying to put something in the list *that no one else has.* Sounds easy, huh? It isn't. The easiest way is to pick up the phone and call a couple of professionals in the area. Ask them: "what do people like me always miss off the list?" or "what would you love to see on the list?" I can almost guarantee they will come up with a unique angle that you would never have discovered by yourself.

Summary

- Cars can be boring, so write about something that's more interesting than the car. Everyone remembers Richard Bremner's beautifully written piece in CAR magazine in 1995 about driving a Ferrari to the Sahara Desert. Not everyone remembers that it was a 512M.
- It's all about the people.
- Don't dismiss listicles. Editors love 'em and so should you.

Photography - delivering the whole package

The biggest mistake new writers make is to assume that when they write about cars, it's the writing that should take centre stage, when the reverse is actually true: a written piece is pictures with words - and a video is radio with pictures. This is why the sections on photography in this might seem disproportionally long to you.

When I was starting out as a wannabe motoring journalist, the best piece of advice I ever received was given by the deputy editor of the best-selling magazine in its class who told me: "don't forget the pictures."

The problem, he told me, is that everyone forgets about images to go with the copy (See, 'images' and 'copy'. You're starting to talk like a pro already) and he just didn't have the budget to send a professional photographer out to do them on the journalist's behalf. The problem was so bad he went on, that he would sometimes publish a second-rate story if the images were good enough. After all, copy can easily be tweaked…

So you need to be able to provide images to back up your work. That's the bad news. The good news is that it really isn't that hard; you'll need equipment but it needn't be expensive (although few activities present a greater opportunity to blow vast amounts of cash quite so quickly as photography if you get carried away) and the skills needed aren't huge, at the beginning at least.

So you need to plan the photographs to go with your writing every bit as carefully as you do the words. This means that you need a camera and the wherewithal to use it properly, which is a huge subject and one I cover in detail in another book. Suffice it to say that you don't need to spend a fortune because the photos that went with my pedal car museum piece were taken on a cheap consumer camera; I just paid attention to the composition and lighting and let the boffins at Canon take care of the rest.

The equipment

Land Rover World used this image across two pages, forming the backbone to a story and it was taken with a Canon G7 boasting just 10.0 megapixels, only a little bit more than an iPhone has these days. Sure, I'd do it differently now I'm more experienced but the point is that it was good enough to be used and it earned me money.

Having said that, the right equipment makes the job easier. After a year or so I was working hard enough to justify moving up to a Canon 7D, relegating the G7 to the role of backup camera, a role it fulfilled admirably until it finally died a couple of years later.

I then got sucked into the world of Canon pro lenses at that point but have never regretted it, despite the cost. An early 70-200mm 2.8 IS, 24-105mm 4.0 IS, and a 50mm 1.4 covered all my early bases and apart from an upgrade to a Canon 6D, they remain the backbone of my kit.

If you don't have a camera, you can get manufacturers' images from websites such as Newspress and/or the car manufacturers' own media websites. These are usually copyright free for editorial use but they're a very poor second to taking your own.

The ten shots every art director needs

If you are reviewing new or secondhand cars for a consumer piece then pretty much every art director or editor is looking for ten basic shots. These are:
- front three-quarter,
- rear three-quarter,
- the side,
- the rear,
- the front,
- the engine bay,
- the boot,

- the front seats,
- rear seats, and (finally),
- the dashboard.

Get the ten main shots in the bag first. Then, and only then, can you start getting creative.

It's all about the light

There are two pieces of advice that I can give you that will raise your photographs to a new level. The first is to stand in front of more interesting things. The second is to think about the light.

Because automotive photography is all about the light. It's not, and never has been, about the car. Some of my best images might be of beautiful cars but it is the light that transforms them into a piece of art, not the metalwork.

This shot of a Maserati works because of the beautiful sunset behind it. Of course the beautiful rear end of the car helps no end, but without the light it wouldn't work even half as well.

It's the same with this shot of a Ford Crown Victoria Interceptor (surely the coolest car name ever?). Moody and haunting, it's the light that makes the image.

The best times to get great light are the first and last hour of the day, the so-called 'Golden Hour'. In fact, I'm being optimistic; the best times to get great light is *sometime* during the first and last hour of *some* days. This elusive moment may only last five minutes, so it's important to be in place and ready. It's not easy, but it is the easiest way to get great shots.

Depth of field

This shot of a Great Wall pickup only works because of the shallow depth of field; the tree is in sharp focus while the vehicle behind it is blurred. This is a very common technique, and is achieved by using your lens wide open, or close to it. For this shot I used an aperture of f4, which is as wide as my Canon 24-105 L f4 lens can go.

In photography, everything is a balance. To expose an image correctly you need to allow a certain amount of light to fall on the camera's sensor; too much and the image will be washed out and over-exposed. Too little and it will be dark and under-exposed. So, all things being equal, a wide open lens will need a short exposure (or a fast shutter speed, as it is the length of time that the camera's shutter is open that determines the exposure length), while a lens that is used with a smaller aperture will need a longer exposure which means a slower shutter speed.

By way of contrast, this image of a red Suzuki was shot at an aperture of f22, because I wanted to get the castle in the background in focus as well as the car. Shot at a focal length of 75mm it required a shutter speed of just 1/180th of a second at ISO400.

Think of it light filling a bucket with water: you can either turn the tap on full (a large aperture) and leave it running for a short period of time (a fast shutter speed), or just open the tap a little bit (a small aperture) and leave it running for longer (a slow shutter speed).

This balance can cause problems. A shallow depth of field means that the shutter is only open for a brief period. This 'freezes' the action, which can be a problem if you are trying to show motion.

Here, a shutter speed of 1/800th of a second was fast enough to freeze the car, keeping the wheels perfectly in focus. As a result it looks like it isn't moving, making it a rather dull shot.

However, for this second shot I used a shutter speed of 1/400th of a second, which gives some motion blur to the wheels, showing that it's moving at high speed.

Still confused? Let me explain.

Shutter speed

For this photograph I wanted to be able to show the movement of the water. To do so, I had to stop the lens right down to f22 (i.e. as closed as it would go) and expose the image for 1.3 seconds. Now, I can reliably hold a camera steady up to a shutter speed of about $1/10^{th}$ of a second if I'm using a lens with image stabilisation; anything longer than that and I need a tripod. I don't like tripods as they're heavy and expensive, but sometimes you just can't get by without one, as in this case.

This gave a beautiful blur to the water but does mean that the whole of the image is in focus. I didn't mind this, but you need to be aware of the need to balance the two settings. There are ways round this problem using Neutral Density (or ND) filters but you don't need to worry about them at this stage of your career.

Of course, getting it wrong can sometimes work to your advantage too.

I grabbed this shot of a Peugeot 2008 at an indoor ski slope when the light was appalling. The combination of handholding the camera at f4, ISO100 and a 0.6 second exposure produced a wonderful image that my editor loved. But it was a complete accident...

The shortcut almost all of us take

Shooting in manual is the Holy Grail and a sign you are a professional photographer rather than a fair weather snapper. However, it takes time to set it up until you are experienced enough to intuitively understand what settings to use.

So most of us choose which is the more important setting and use that. So if I want to control the depth of field, I'll put my camera on 'aperture priority' and dial in the aperture setting I want. The camera will then set the ISO and shutter speed automatically.

If I'm shooting a moving car and want to either blur the background when I'm panning with a slow shutter speed or freeze the action with a fast shutter speed, I'll put the camera in 'shutter priority' and set it, leaving the camera to figure out which ISO and aperture to use to expose correctly.

Summary

- It's not about the equipment; if you remember nothing else, remember that. An iPhone or Smartphone will do at a pinch and a £300 digital camera will do an excellent job if you can afford one.

- Buy James Mann's book ***How To Photograph Cars***. It isn't cheap, but it is very good.

Automotive Photography
by James Neale

James Neale is a ridiculously young and ridiculously talented commercial photography that I've worked with for years. He's brilliant at working under pressure and all the images in this piece were taken in minutes, rather than hours.

As a photographer I get to go to some amazing places and photograph some amazing people. I love every second of my job and I feel very lucky to be doing something that I enjoy. As a business I cover many different areas, including weddings, portraits, commercial and photography training but my favourite area is automotive photography.

I was once told that your best work comes from the area of photography that you enjoy the most and that's certainly been proven right when I was awarded Commercial Photographer of the Year 2011 by Professional Photographer Magazine for my picture of the Jaguar XF.

Photographing cars has always interested me; I suppose you could say they turn me on photographically. The smooth reflective body, the beautifully crafted lines and curves, the chrome badges and trim, all stand out to me. When I look at a car I see the potential of these details, in images.

Going from a hobby photographer to a professional, I sometimes feel the need to get out with the camera and do my own thing, rather than what the client wants, and cars are my passion. So here are some basics to help you to go out and create some amazing automotive shots.

Location, location, location

The first thing I do when it comes to shooting cars is to find a suitable location. The location is such a key part of the photograph that I'm constantly scoping out new and interesting places so that when I do get the opportunity to head out with a car, I don't have to drive about aimlessly wasting time.

I use two pieces of technology to help with this. Firstly is my trusty iPhone: If I'm out on my travels and I come across somewhere that I think will look good for a shoot I will take a quick snap and the phone marks the GPS location for me to help find it again a few months later. The other is Google street view, a brilliant concept that makes it quick and easy to walk around streets and villages without leaving the comfort of my office to see if there are any interesting places there.

Getting the position of the car right

Once you're at your location with the car, the first thing is to get it positioned properly. Park the car in the area you want to shoot it in and then take a step back and look around the car. Make sure there are no distracting objects, signs, rubbish around and behind the car. A lot of photographers fail to do this and then have to spend time removing these using Photoshop later.

Turn the wheels a little bit to one side. I always find that when I'm shooting a car it's always nice to have the wheels turned so they are facing you as I think it just gives the car a better stance. The only exception to this is when you are side on to it when the wheels need to be straight.

Choosing the best angle to shoot at

This is down to the effect you want to have on the final picture. Shooting from a very low angle can give a totally different look to the image than just shooting from standing position. I always look through the viewfinder and move around until I see the shot I want.

Reflections can look great if what is being reflected is interesting or fits the style of the picture but remember not to capture yourself in reflections, one of the greatest problems in automotive photography!

Lighting

Lighting conditions will have a big effect on the final image and I find the best time to shoot cars is on cloudy days because the clouds will act as large softbox and help defuse the light.

Obviously there are going to be times when you want to shoot during bright sunlight and in these situations you are going to have to work with the light and position the car where the light reflections look best.

Circular polarizing filters will help with the reduction of unwanted reflections and glare from the sun, making one a must-have accessory for your kit bag.

If you want to remove all reflections from the car, you need to set the camera up on a tripod and take a series of pictures, turning the polarizing filter for each shot before blending them together using Photoshop. This is a lengthy process and takes time.

Sometimes though I don't think its really necessary. With this Bentley Continental I only had 15 minutes to get a full range of shots and would never have had the time to do this for every angle and shot. Just work with the light and use the reflections to show off the beautiful lines of the car.

Action shots

Action shots are a great way to create some stunning images and there are a few ways to create them.

Panning is where you stand on the side of the road and as the car passes you, you follow it with the camera. You need to keep the focus point on the same position on the car, shoot in Shutter Priority and choose a speed of around 1/30 sec to begin with. With some practice you will get some great shots where the wheels and the background will blur but the body of the car will be nice and sharp. You will need to turn your camera's settings to Continuous Focusing so that it constantly re-focuses as the distance between you and the car changes.

Another way to do this is to shoot from another car. Both cars need to be travelling at the same speed, and if you keep the shutter speed low you should be able to get some amazing shots that will add some speed and movement to the image.

Processing in Photoshop

I run all my shots through Photoshop to give them that little something extra, although the amount of editing involved is not generally that great.

First, I will look to see if any straightening or cropping is needed before I look at the colours in the picture. With darker cars I normally will wash out a lot of the colour in the background to help make the car stand out. For this I use the Sponge tool and just desaturate the affected areas. Then it's just a case of using the burn tool to darken sky to give the picture the moody look that I like. You can use some contrast to really emphasize this look.

So there you have it, hopefully a few hints and tips that you can use to improve your automotive photography. The main thing that will really improve your photography though is practice because I don't think you ever stop learning. With every shoot I do, I always improve on the one before.

Thanks for reading.

James Neale
James Neale Photography
http://www.jamesnealephotography.com

All photographs in this section are © James Neale

Video

Before you start recording your own videos, you will need some extra equipment. Not much, but some and it'll come to around £500. No way round that, I'm afraid, unless you're going to go down the iPhone route. Which you're not, are you?

Equipment

Your DSLR is a miracle of modern consumerism, offering far higher quality images than any of us really need. It'll deliver ten-frames a second of ultra-high definition JPEGs with nigh spot-on white balance, focus and exposure under just about any conditions you're likely to encounter. If all else fails you can stick it on its automatic setting and it'll churn technically acceptable images until the battery runs dry or you run out of memory, whichever happens first.

Video is a whole different ball game, essentially because your DSLRs video mode is an afterthought, piggybacking its photographic capability by shooting 30 frames a second (or whatever frame rate you choose) to produce a film.

The problems start with the amazing autofocus lens you rely on so much. When you're shooting video it'll hunt between focal points, making an annoying noise to accompany the annoying focus shift. So you need to manually focus your lens, which means you need a hood loupe so you can see what you're supposed to be focusing on. I use a £100 Hoodman Hoodloupe, which gets the job done well enough for my needs.

A tripod, with a hydraulic pan-and-tilt head, should be on your shopping list too. I picked up a sturdy pro-video one on eBay for £40. It's ugly and heavy (oh boy, is it heavy) but it was cheap and it's easily good enough for what I shoot.

You'll need two microphones: a small one with a long cable for when you're interviewing and a larger, directional microphone that mounts in your DSLR's hot shoe for more general work. I use a Røde VideoMic Pro in my hot shoe, which retails at around £150 and a Lavalier lapel microphone from the same company for interviewing. It also costs around £150, which might seem a lot, but the sound quality on your films is easily as important, if not more so, than the pictures. Remember: video is just radio with pictures.

You need to buy, and become familiar with using, a set of filters to be able to maintain the correct exposure. I use Cokin filters, which are cheap and get the job done with no fuss. A kit comprising three neutral density graduated filters (ND Grads) and three neutral density (ND) filters and a filter holder set me back under £50.

A Follow Focus (a series of large wheels that enable more accurate focusing, as well as the ability to quickly move between pre-determined points, say from the presenter to the car) costs a similar amount but is definitely a luxury rather than an essential.

That's it for the equipment, now for the technique...

Technique

To go into the detail of the videographers job is beyond a dedicated book, much less one chapter in a book as wide-ranging as this one! However, here are some pointers that have stood me in good stead:

- Plan your shoot before you turn the camera on. You need to know what you're trying to achieve before you try and achieve it. It's true that some of your best footage will come about by accident but that'll only work as part of a structured shoot.
- Everyone loves the shallow depth of field that DSLR lens can give. However, it can be seen as a bit *passé* now, so don't rely on it as your only technique.

- Similarly, don't go overboard on the special effects in the editing studio. Simple is usually better.
- Shoot in small bursts. You want plenty of angle changes, perspectives and alternative views. Aim for 50% close-ups, 25% mid-range, and 25% long-range shots as a guide when you're setting out.
- The corollary of that is to go steady with your camera angles when you are videoing an interview. The person should be the hero of the shot.
- Use a tripod whenever you can. Shaky shots just look shaky, not arty.
- Always be mindful of the soundtrack. Radio, with pictures, yes?

As ever, the best advice is to get professional training from an expert. I spent a day and a few hundred pounds with Line and Light (http://www.lineandlight.co.uk/) and learned far more in one day than I ever thought possible.

Summary

- You need to spend £500 or so to turn your DSLR into a proper video camera.
- Plan your story thoroughly before you start shooting it.
- Don't go overboard on the special effects.

Evaluating a car

Before you even think about getting behind the wheel of a car buy yourself a nice notebook and a pen that feels good in the hand and carry them everywhere with you. After all, you're a writer so you're supposed to write, aren't you?

Ideas, thoughts, sounds and smells are all grist to the mill and if you don't make a note, you will forget them. Never assume you will remember everything. You won't. Trust me.

Getting hold of a car from the press fleet

Getting hold of cars to test is easy once you're established but it's almost impossible when you're just starting out. That's OK, because there are a thousand different stories you can write without getting anywhere near a new car. As James Ruppert, the author of a number of books on cars and the car industry, the founding editor of Free Car Mag (http://www.freecarmag.co.uk/), and the brains behind the Bangernomics movement put it to me:

> *"The only qualification to be a writer is to be able to write. Stuff cars. You should be able to make a trip to shops amusing. Essentially you need to be Bill Bryson and then turn your attention to motors."*

So forget about writing about new cars for the time being (the money's rubbish anyway) and hone your craft without them.

Having said that, you will, at some point, be asked to write a car review and to do that you need access to new cars. Luckily, car manufacturers have a vested interest in letting motoring journalists drive their cars (but a finely honed nose for bullshit), so honesty is your best bet.

Try the smaller manufacturers first; there is no point in approaching Ferrari or Porsche until you're established. Besides, it's much easier to sell copy on a small family hatchback or MPV than it is on a supercar.

Tell them who you are and what you're trying to achieve in an email initially, followed up with a phone call if you haven't heard anything after a week or so. They'll generally be extremely helpful and positive and while they might not lend you a car initially (although some will) they will definitely guide you towards alternative ways to get you into one of their cars.

Other ways? Yes, remember I said you should keep a close eye on **the SMMT** website? Every year they run three test days where the UK's car manufacturers assemble with hundreds of shiny new cars for you to drive. The biggest, and best, is held at Milbrook Proving Ground in Bedfordshire but there are regional ones held in the north and south of the country too. This is an ideal opportunity to drive a number of cars in a day helping you build that mental databank you'll come to rely on everyday of your working life.

Most manufacturers also run media drive days when they bring their press fleet along and let you loose in them. This is, again, a great way to build knowledge and, more importantly, relationships.

Press car etiquette

The manufacturer has just lent you a car worth tens of thousands of pounds, so treat it well. That means not ragging it senseless, keeping it relatively clean and not damaging it. None of that is rocket science but you'd be amazed at how many of your colleagues abuse the cars mercilessly, all in the name of 'reviewing' them.

But accidents do happen and if you scrape, scratch, or otherwise damage the car – no matter how - you have no choice but to pick up the phone to the press fleet manager to tell them about it. Straightaway. Stuff happens and they won't mind at all as long as it wasn't done as a result of your recklessness. They will mind if you don't tell them about it and the first they hear is when the press fleet garage phones them to tell them that their press car is off the road and can't be used until it's repaired. This will annoy everyone concerned, especially the poor journalist whose car loan gets cancelled because you didn't give the garage enough notice to get it repaired in time.

The men and women who deliver your car to your door do a fantastic job and are some of the nicest and most interesting people in the business so always offer to take them to the nearest train station or bus stop - and collect them when they return in a week's time. Always leave them at least a quarter of a tank of fuel, too; to do anything else is mean-spirited and petty. Many journalists don't do this and make every effort to drain every last drop. Guess which group the press fleet managers think better of?

Always ask for a specification sheet for any press car (there will probably be one in the glovebox and attached to the email confirming the press car booking) you drive. Double-check the facts and figures on it against the manufacturer's website and if in doubt, double-check any anomalies with the press office; it's your responsibility to get it right, not theirs.

Use social media to your advantage during the loan, too. Take lots of photographs and post them across your platforms, tagging the manufacturer and any local dealers. It's all good advertising and you'll be surprised at how many followers and likes you can get from a re-tweet or share.

Finally, always send links to published work or photocopies of anything in a newspaper or magazine. This is how the PR people judge how cost effective the loan has been, and this is the key to getting a steady stream of cars to review.

Driving a car to evaluate it

Driving a car to evaluate it is not the same as ragging it senseless on your favourite stretch of B-road to the backbeat of your favourite soundtrack: while the latter is enormous fun it generally tells you the square root of nothing about how a car handles and drives.

As a professional motoring journalist your job is to rule yourself out of the equation by driving every car in a consistent and repeatable way so you can report objectively and independently on the car's dynamic behaviour.

The best £1,000 I ever spent was a day with Colin Hoad of Cat Driver Training (http://www.catdrivertraining.co.uk/) and I'm not alone in thinking that. While Colin is too modest to tell you so himself, he's trained a few of us over the years, including quite a few guys you will have heard of and read. If you can beg, steal, or borrow the money, you should go and spend a day with him. Tell him what you want out of the day and he will tailor it to suit.

However, I accept that £1,000 is a lot of money and while I can't think of anything better to invest that sort of sum in you can do a pretty good job of evaluating any car using a few simple techniques.

Before you climb in take a good look at the car. How are you going to describe it to someone who hasn't seen it yet? Does it look lithe, purposeful, awkward, sleek, or staid? Does it look fit-for-purpose or just plain boring? Is it an improvement over the outgoing model? If so, why?

Now get into it. Try and get comfortable behind the wheel. Sit in the back. Try folding the rear seats. Use the car like an owner would. You're not writing about a family MPV from your perspective, you're trying to get into the mindset of a stressed mum of three who's struggling with half-a-dozen bags of shopping as she's trying to corral her brood.

Then start it up, and listen to it. Is it loud or quiet? If it's loud is it a good loud or an intrusive one; what is the *quality* of the noise?

Pull away; how are the clutch, gear-change, and steering?
When it's safe to do so brake to a halt from a low speed. How are the brakes? Progressive or overly sharp? Good initial bite or a long, dead pedal?

Try cornering in it: evaluate how it enters the corner, then how it feels mid-corner and finally how it is on the exit. Be consistent when you're cornering: use a steady state throttle (i.e. keep it in one position) and single-input steering (look towards the end of the bend and try not to keep adding and subtracting steering lock) will let you feel what the car is doing through a corner – and will do so reliably.

Ask yourself if you're *enjoying* it? If so, analyse *why* because you can't very well simply write that you enjoyed yourself, can you?

Try some acceleration tests from rest and then through the gears as if you are overtaking slower traffic. How does it feel? Where is the power? How is the gearchange? Can you rush it or do you need to be smooth. Is it fighting you or does it slip through the gate easily?

Take the car to a higher speed. Is it quiet? If not, where is the noise coming from: wind, tyres, road, engine or a combination of all three?

Again, when it's safe to do so try braking to a halt from a higher speed; do the brakes fade or stay firm? Judder or stay smooth?

Now pull up somewhere and grab a coffee while you write down your initial feelings and impressions. Don't worry about making whole sentences because brief notes will do just fine at this stage.

Wash the car if you can; seriously, there is no better way to get a deep understanding of the car's design.

Now get out and drive it again and double-check your initial impressions. Try and benchmark it against the competition, the cars you've previously driven. (Don't worry, you'll quickly build up a mental bank of all the key players and where they fit in the hierarchy.)

Think about the 'hook' for your story. Have you got one yet? If not get out and drive it some more…

Getting it all down on paper

Once you've driven the car and got your hook it's time to get behind the keyboard and make like a writer.

Research your car's statistics and read through the press pack the manufacturer has given you. Most of it will be PR puff but there will be some good stuff in there but make sure you don't fall for the hyperbole or quote whole chunks out of it. Oh, and whatever you do, don't read anyone else's road tests just yet. You will, but not now. Now is the time for unfettered, influence-free objectivity.

Now write your initial review. Get it all down: how it drives; whether the boot is big enough; whether the pricing is competitive; have the changes the manufacturer claims to have made actually made a difference over the old model or is it merely marketing guff written to persuade people to change their car more frequently?

Be honest, but not rude. Few cars are completely devoid of charm and you won't get away with gratuitous abuse. So while it's fair to benchmark a car's poor ride against that of its competitors, it's unfair to start talking about shattered spines.

Remember the target market for the car too. Not everyone cares about handling like you and I do, and even fewer drivers drop the clutch at 7,000rpm to get the very best standing start acceleration. Lots of people do care about the boring stuff like fuel consumption, residual values and boot space.

Once you've got it all committed to paper you can hit the Internet to find out what other people are saying. If you are out of step is that because you've got it wrong or because they have? If you think they've been too accommodating you might be right; an awful lot of semi-professional motoring writers (the ones who give their copy away for free in return for the loan of a press car or an invitation to a new car launch being held in sunnier climes) will write uncomplicated, unrelentingly positive waffle. Don't be like them. You're better than that.

Honing your skills

Writing reviews and then comparing your impressions with what the rest of the industry is saying is a great way of honing your analytical skills. Try and attend an SMMT Test Day, or one of the regional days run by the car manufacturers, and drive half-a-dozen cars. Take copious notes and then write your review. Don't worry too much about grammar, spelling and sentence construction too much at this point.

The object of the exercise is to compare your impressions with those of a few motoring writers that you respect. Are you broadly in line with their findings? If not, why? It could be that your experiential database is too small at this point, leading you to over-estimate how good a car is. (In fact, now that I think of it, avoiding superlatives full stop isn't a bad rule.)

Polishing

Now polish. The biggest problem the industry faces is an increasing inability to write grammatically. You might think that grammar doesn't matter any more. You're wrong. It does. So read, and re-read people whose work you admire and note how their stories are underpinned by good grammar. Take liberties with sentence structure by all means. Even start a sentence with an 'and' or a 'but' if you must.

Hell, you can even invent words if you're talented enough (something the late Russell Bulgin was especially good at) but please get the basics right, so when you break grammatical rules the reader knows you are doing it consciously and not because you're an ill-educated lout.

Summary

- Keep your notes and notebooks forever. Forever, y'hear?
- Obey most of the grammatical rules. Companies are always singular ('it') not plural ('they') for example, and if you don't know when and where to use 'their', 'there', and 'they're' you need to find out! On the other hand, start as many sentences with 'and' and 'but' as you like.
- Double-check everything. Then check it again.

Your first car launch

For many of us, attending our first new car launch is a rite of passage, a sign that we've arrived. Of course, it's perfectly possible to be a *bona fida* motoring journalist or writer without ever attending one. But the only people who really think that are those who have been to dozens of them already.

So, attending your first launch event is a real milestone in your writing career, so you'd better not mess it up, had you?

What will happen

You will get your invitation by email. By all means revel in the moment but don't wait for too long before replying because spaces will be limited and if you hesitate, you might just lose your place.

So reply as quickly as you can and put it in your diary. There are few worse phone calls to receive than one from a very nice PR asking what time you will be arriving at an event you'd forgotten all about. Not that I've ever done that you understand...

You will be offered a train ticket or plane flight depending on distance. You're good to go either way because you've got your kit packed in your overnight bag and laptop case, enabling you to travel light and fast; no checking huge suitcases into the hold of the plane for you.

A member of the PR team will greet you when you arrive. The really good ones will know who you are, even if you've never met them before. The good ones will pretend, while everyone else will ask.

The usual format is to settle into your room before joining everyone else for pre-dinner drinks. This is nerve-wracking because you probably won't know anyone at first. Nonetheless, try and make the effort to join in a few conversations anyway, although being in a group of journalists is one of the few social occasions when using your phone to update social media is not seen as rude...

Dinner will be loud, informal, and full of outrageous stories. Most don't talk about the automotive business or models they've driven (I still remember one grizzled, living legend, joining me outside for a cigar, complaining loudly that he was sitting with a bunch of boring bastards who only wanted to talk about *cars*!), which can seem a bit odd at first. But we're a friendly bunch and alcohol is a great social lubricant.

(Although you may well be breathalysed the next morning before you're allowed to drive, so take it easy, won't you?)

Sharing a car

You'll need to pair up with another journalist in the morning, which isn't as awkward as it sounds as there is no better way to make new friends than to be stuck in a car with a stranger for eight hours. And anyway, it gives you a captive audience to tap for information, doesn't it?

Most manufacturers use sat-nav to navigate the driving route but a few still use written books giving directions calibrated against the odometer. You will make a mistake and probably get lost if you are navigating using the latter. Please don't worry when that happens, it's almost inevitable and we've all done it.

By way of contrast, not calling out the location of a speed camera on the route - either from the notes or by spotting one in the distance - to the driver is unforgiveable. You have been warned.

Taking notes

Almost everyone takes notes during the press conference (which will be held either the night before or in the morning before you get into the cars) but hardly anyone takes notes of notes of what the car is like to drive. That's because they've got brilliant memories honed by years of experience. You haven't, so take notes. No one will think you're weird, I promise.

A warning

On my first launch (the Audi A1, if you're interested) the most common piece of advice I was given (by a factor of about ten) was: *"don't bite the hand that feeds you."* That disgusted and revolted me as much then as it does now. The industry is full of people who give their work away for free and so have a vested interest in writing only nice things (or mildly critical things if they've woken up feeling especially angst-ridden) about a car to ensure the gravy train doesn't grind to a halt.

Don't be like them. If you are, no one will respect you, least of all your peers and readers. You won't like yourself much, either.

On the other hand, you can draw solace, of a sort, from the situation. An awful lot of the people there don't know half as much about cars as they pretend, many of them being generalist journalists who cover cars in their own time as a perk.

This means you should never feel inferior in their company. (On the other hand, the full-time professional motoring journalists who write for the specialist magazines, websites and newspapers are awesomely knowledgeable and if they express an opinion, it's probably worth listening to.)

Post-launch

Get your notes into order as soon as you can; the train ride or flight home is an ideal time to consolidate them and get your thoughts about the car in order.

Then write up your review (which I've covered in the previous chapter on Evaluating a Car) post it online or email it to your editor and relax.

Send a PDF of the pages or a website link to the PR team when it's published. They gauge your worth (my words, not theirs) by the audience you reach. They won't be overly concerned by constructive, accurate criticism but they will be if they invite you to events and you don't write a word about them.

Summary

- Don't be afraid to ask other journalists what their impressions are of the car you're driving.
- Send the PR team copies of what you've written.
- Enjoy yourself! After all, it's what you always dreamed of, isn't it?

Your first race meeting or motor show

I attended a lot of race meetings and motor shows in the early days. Not because anyone was paying me to be there but to enable me to build up a supply of stock images that I could use elsewhere later in my career. So, if you want a photo of a stack of slick racing tyres, or a fuel can, or a Formula One car at speed, or a concours Bristol 411 I'm your man. (And yes, they've all been sold as stock photography or come in handy for features I've written years later.)

Of course, you might get lucky and find someone willing to pay you, in which case you're doing better than I ever have. Either way, this is what you need to know.

Signing on

Your first job is to find the media tent or suite and sign on with them. This is no hardship because they'll usually have coffee, bacon rolls and free Wi-Fi. And toilets. (When you get to my age you learn to find the toilets pretty damned fast.)

Photographers' vests

If you're taking photographs and want trackside access you'll need to provide a certificate demonstrating that you have £5,000,000 of third-party liability insurance before they'll give you your photographers' vest. It's not expensive but it might just save you from personal bankruptcy when an idiot trips over your camera bag one day.

The photographers' vest is just a sleeveless fluorescent jacket with 'media' or 'press' on the back, which makes you look the part and lets you root around in places the public can't.

The marshals

Marshals are volunteers who give up their time in order to get wet, bored and abused by members of the public who have no appreciation of how dangerous motorsport can be and can't understand why they are being asked to move to a safer place by a chap or chapess in bright clothing.

Don't be one of them. If they ask you to move, then you must move. Immediately and without question. If you have a photographers' vest, then ask where you can stand. They won't be difficult about it and might even point you to a corner where the big spins tend to happen. And they always have great big flasks of coffee and it can get cold out there…

Get in close

Being a journalist gives you the right – no, the obligation – to be nosy. So get up close and personal and ask questions. You don't need to pretend to be Jeremy Paxman because you will catch more flies with honey than vinegar. Be nice, be interested, and ask questions. Offer them your card and ask for theirs. Send them some of the photos you've taken. Follow them on Twitter or Instagram. Build a relationship with them because they're interesting and funny and good company. In return you might just get access to events and people and situations you would never have dreamed were possible.

Post-event

Send the event's PR team website links and PDFs of your work covering the event. If you haven't got any, then email them and thank them for giving you access. This job is about being nice whenever you can. Remember that.

Summary

- If you want to get trackside, you'll need public liability insurance.
- Be nosy. It's your obligation and without it your readers can't live vicariously through you.
- Be nice. You're a journalist and that means you've got the profession's reputation in your hands every time you identity yourself as one of us.

Interviewing

Interviewing someone is one of the more fascinating aspects of our job (remember: it's all about the people, right?) but it's more time consuming than you imagine, so you need to be prepared to make it work for you.

The three stages of every interview

I have a three-stage plan that's never let me down:

1. Before you interview anyone you need to do your research. Read up on them, ask other people about them and watch them interact with others if you can. I interviewed the head of a well-known car manufacturer once and he was without doubt the rudest, most unpleasant man I'd spoken to since becoming a motoring journalist – but that was OK because he was like that with everyone. If I hadn't asked questions and watched him before speaking to him his attitude might

have thrown me and turned an unpleasant experience into a full-blown disaster.

© Griffin Technology

2. Record everything. I use a small Olympus digital voice recorder that cost me under £30 and while it has never let me down I like to have a back up in the form of a second recording on my iPhone. I use iTalk from Griffin Technology, a brilliantly intuitive app that gives me peace of mind. I've never had to rely on it but it'll save my bacon one day, I'm sure. I also take handwritten notes on the key points that I use later to guide me to the more interesting portions of the interview. (It also gives you a few moments of breathing space if you lose your train of thought!)

3. After you've written up the interview – a process that takes an awful lot longer than you can imagine - why not send a draft to the person you've just interviewed for them to check it for accuracy? Be clear you are not asking them to approve the angle or editorial slant, just the accuracy of their words and thoughts.

Sometimes you'll be asked if something can be 'off the record' or held under the 'Chatham House Rule'. This means the person you're talking to is happy to tell you something but doesn't want it attributing to them. I generally agree, figuring it's better to know something and not be able to use it than to not know in the first place.

Others feel differently and this is one of the minefields you'll need to negotiate on your own but interviewing, like social media, is about building relationships and once people learn that they can trust you they'll lead you into some very interesting places.

Summary

Accurate notes could be the difference between having an unhappy interviewee or being sued for libel. If they said it and you reported it accurately then it's defensible, although whether you should have written it is a matter for you and your conscience...

Chatham House Rule
/ˌtʃatəm haʊs ˈruːl/

noun BRITISH

a rule or principle according to which information disclosed during a meeting may be reported by those present, but the source of that information may not be explicitly or implicitly identified.
"the conference was held under the Chatham House Rule"

Definition courtesy of Google

The equipment you need

At its most basic, all a motoring journalist needs is a pen and a scrap of paper. Well, in theory, anyway. The reality is that you do need a certain of equipment to be competitive; this is what I use.

Computers

I use an Apple Mac Pro in the office for two reasons: first, I can't get on with laptops with their fiddly little screens. It's a generational thing, I'm sure and, of course, they have their place – you'll often find me hunched over one in an airport departure lounge – but for the day-to-day work I prefer something bigger, hence my Apple Mac Pro with a 30" Cinema Display. It's easily powerful enough for intensive video and photo editing and almost infinitely expandable and upgradeable.

Extravagant? Not really, because I paid the same for it as you would for a middling Apple laptop as I bought it secondhand from a lovely chap called Jon Bradbury, the owner of Bramley Computers (http://bramley-computers.co.uk/). He now looks after all my Apple products and has saved me a fortune over the years. He could do the same for you.

I also have an old 13" Apple MacBook Pro for use when I'm travelling. I don't use it much but when I do it's a lifesaver, enabling me to make last-minute changes at the behest of an editor or to write a breaking-news story.

My laptop is supplemented with an iPad Mini for reading and watching videos in hotel rooms and on planes. I also use it for basic video editing on the rare occasion that I don't have my laptop.

Phone

© Apple

My iPhone6 is invaluable, not least for taking brilliant photos that I can upload on my social media platforms with the minimum of fuss. It also has a few basic apps on it that make life so much easier. These include:

- Snapseed for basic photo editing. Ditto Photoshop Express (PS Express).
- FiLMiC Pro for the rare occasions when I use my iPhone to record a separate soundtrack for video.
- CoPilot GPS, still the best sat-nav app ever designed and useful when I'm in a car without a factory system.
- RoadPilot, to help me dodge speed cameras.

- Dynolicious, a fun app that lets me play around in a safe environment to test a review car's G-force under braking, acceleration, and cornering as well as its acceleration. It should NEVER be used on the road.
- Harry's LapTimer, again, very useful on a track but no use anywhere else.

Camera

© Canon

I use a Canon 6D paired with a 24-105mm f4 L lens and a circular polarizing filter. With two 32GB memory cards and a couple of spare batteries I've got a kit that will shoot 99% of the shots I need and last for a week or so into the bargain without having to pack a battery charger. I keep it all in a LowePro TopLoader Zoom bag.

Laptop bag

The whole lot is carted around in a LowePro Urban Reporter 250 bag, along with a couple of notebooks, half-a-dozen pens, a small, telescopic umbrella, an Olympus VN-8600 digital voice recorder with a lapel microphone and an inline telephone microphone (for telephone interviews), and an emergency power supply for my iPhone and iPad. Plus the relevant charging and connecting cables and some spare AAA batteries.

Overnight bag

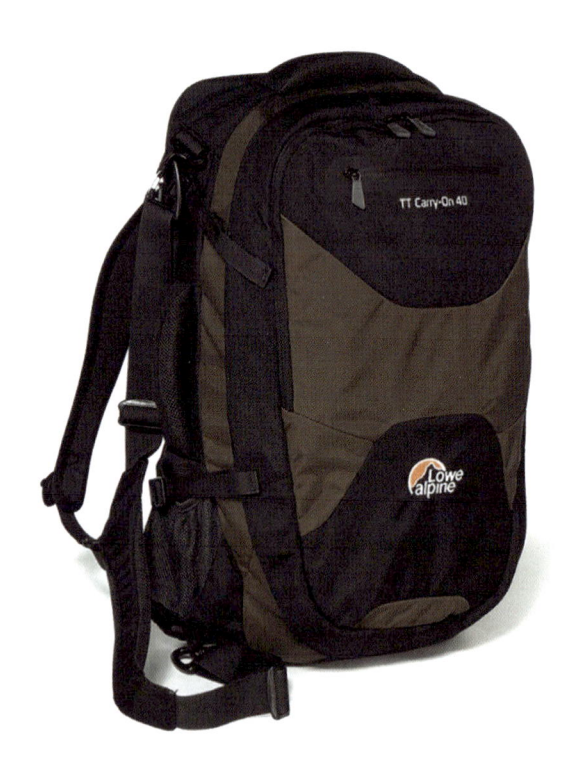

© Lowe Alpine

My overnight bag is the simply brilliant Lowe Alpine TT Carry-On 40, which is small enough to be accrued on any airplane as hand luggage but big enough to fit in a week's worth of clothing. Between my TT Carry-On and my Urban Reporter bag I never have to check my luggage into the hold, saving me time and stress.

And no, before you ask, I'm not recommending any of these products because I've been given free samples: I've paid for them all out of my own pocket.

Copyright

Copyright is one of the least understood aspects of our profession but it's one of the most important. It's a huge subject that is far too big to cover comprehensively in a book of this kind but I'll try and cover the stuff that's most important to you as you start your writing career. Further information can be found on the Internet, but as you're a writer you should be buying a copy of *The Writers' and Artists' Yearbook* anyway and it has a number of articles that delve deeper into the subject.

The UK government has a very good guide to assigning copyright too: https://www.gov.uk/government/publications/copyright-notice-assignment-of-copyright.

What exactly are you selling?

Simply put, you are not selling your words or photographs, you are selling a licence for people to use them; in the United Kingdom the copyright automatically belongs to you (other countries can vary) and will continue to do so until you grant it to someone else. Which you will rarely do, of course.

So, when you sell an article to a newspaper, magazine, website, or book, you are selling the right for that one outlet to publish the feature. That might be an exclusive right (i.e. you can't then sell the same words and images to anyone else, although you can, of course, re-write it so it's a completely different article and sell that…) or a qualified right. A qualified right is the right for them to publish the article once in a magazine, for example. If the publisher then wants to publish it online on its website it will need to agree that with you separately, hopefully for another fee.

Life is rarely that simple, however. You generally sell the rights to a publisher for all usage. I include the details of what I'm selling on the invoice that is submitted at the same time as the completed work. It doesn't have to be complicated: just have a column on your invoice that tells the client what they're buying. Typically I'll put 'magazine and website' that enables the client to understand clearly what they're buying.

What if it all goes wrong?

What if, despite your best efforts, the client uses the article on its website when he or she only paid you to use it in a magazine? As ever, communication is the key here. It's happened to me and the article was withdrawn immediately and because I spoke to the group editor (rather than the editor of the regional magazine that I usually dealt with) - and the whole conversation was conciliatory rather than confrontational - I got more features commissioned from her for to be used across the whole magazine group.

But you will come across some people who just ignore your emails and phone calls, hoping you'll just go away. Your tolerance levels and patience might be greater than mine but I've rarely found it worth pursuing.

I just write it off to experience and vow never to work with them again – unless they pay me far more than they did the first time to account for the aggravation they caused me.

Pitching your work

As an established professional motoring writer you'll pitch your story before you write a single word because you don't want to waste hours or days getting a story only to find you can't sell it. As a newbie though, you'll sometimes have to write it first and pray that someone wants it. (Of course, if it's for your blog, then you can publish whatever you like. That's the joy of being your own editor!)

Pitching a story is the bit we all hate. Every single one of us. It's often said that writers are the most insecure of all the professions and I suspect it's true; every rejection feels personal and a direct insult to your abilities. I could tell you that that's nonsense but you won't believe me when it happens.

Researching your pitch

The key to a good pitch is research. Read the magazine or website you intend to pitch to get a feel for its house style. Consumer magazines won't be interested in a long-form piece on the collapse of the Chinese supply chain, and a Buzzfeed-style website won't want a review of the latest incarnation of the Porsche 911.

However, the former might well be interested in a short piece on the impact the collapse will have on the retail price of new cars and the residual value of older models, while a listicle website might love something on the 911s evolution over the years or an infographic showing how those changes have altered the shape of the car over the past five decades.

Once you've got a half-decent idea that might suit a particular outlet it's time to Google its website to make sure it hasn't published something similar in the near past. Assuming it hasn't you should then Google its competitors to make sure none of them has done anything similar too.

Originality is hard, but once you've got it you could be on to a winner.

What format to pitch in

So, how should you pitch an idea? I prefer to do so via email as it gives the editor time to read it when he or she isn't busy. I start by introducing myself briefly before going on to tell them what I'd like to sell them. You should, ideally, be able to describe it in one sentence, two at the most. They're busy people and won't read anything that is too long-winded. But your idea needs space to breath, so expand a little into another paragraph or two. If they like what you're saying they'll read more, which is why the first, brief outline is so important.

Close by telling them who you'll be interviewing to flesh out the piece (if it's exclusive access that's even better…) and explain that you can provide images to go with it before asking them if there is a good time to call them to discuss it further. Add your phone number, blog name, and social media names at the bottom - and don't press send until you've double-checked it for typos.

The follow-up

You'll wait and wait and you won't hear a thing. This is because editors are busy and they get dozens of emails like yours every day of the week. So you've got to get creative. Be original. Pitch an even crazier story. Pitch something they can't get anywhere else. Keep pitching, but only pitch one idea at a time to one outlet. One of the worst mistakes you can make is to get two lots of editors excited about a potential article, only to have to let one of them down.

They'll still ignore you. But keep going. I got my best-ever gig through sheer persistence but the acceptance email got lost in the ether and if I hadn't have chased it they'd have thought I wasn't interested and given it to a colleague. Now I love some of my colleagues like brothers but that was my gig, not theirs.

However, if you keep harassing them they'll get very annoyed and never employ you as long as there is air in their lungs; three emails is probably enough. Anything more is harassment.

One to consider

Another, high-risk, way to get your work in front of an editor is to write and photograph the whole thing first and send it to them up-front. It means a lot of work is potentially going to be wasted but it does allow him or her to see the quality of your work before committing money and space to an unknown quantity.

I've done it on a few occasions and sometimes it's paid off and sometimes it hasn't. It's a risk but probably one worth taking in the early stages of your career. Even if it doesn't end up appearing in print or pixels it's all good experience and no time spent writing anything is ever wasted.

Pricing your work

Ah, the thorny question of how much to charge. In 2015 the rates vary massively but 10 pence per word is a good rate and one pound a word is very good. I've had two pounds a word on a few occasions and that felt like I was winning.

Most publications and websites don't pay by the word, though. Payment for an article is by far the norm, which makes it harder to price a piece of work, especially when you've agreed a price and the editor comes back to you and asks for another 500 words but doesn't want to pay you any more money. (I sucked it up and delivered the new word count for the old rate as it was a prestigious outlet. I'm still not sure I did the right thing.)

The rate for reviews of new cars are pitifully low – if you can get anyone to pay in the first place given the plethora of 'journalists' out there who'll give their copy away. So, £75 for a 750-1,000 word review of a new car is a good rate, but be prepared to accept much less; I've heard the figure of £25 being bandied about on more than one occasion, which won't even pay for the airport car-park.

See, you're never going to get rich, are you?

Working for free

You'll probably have to work for free initially too, which is good experience for when you do start to get paid, because you'll only ever earn a pittance. Contact car magazines, websites, and blogs offering to work as an unpaid intern for a week or so. Link to your blog, so they can see the quality of your writing. If you are successful you'll get contacts out of it, bylines, and experience.

I learned more writing news articles for a well-known motoring outlet than anything else I have done. If nothing else, you'll realise that writing about a mid-term facelift of a nondescript car is a soul-destroying experience but it is one that you'll have to do several times a week. This work experience will help you get a paid gig, after which you'll be moving through the industry like a shark.

Note what I wrote in that last sentence. The unpaid work will help you get a paid job. As in someone will pay you for your work. Please, please don't get sucked into giving your work away for free like so may do. Swapping your talent and hard work for a free car once a week and the odd all-expenses-paid oversees jaunt might seem an attractive deal but it isn't. Not only are you better than that by doing so you are killing the very industry you are trying to join.

On a recent car launch I estimated that well over half of the 'journalists' there weren't getting paid for their time. Just because they lack the self-respect and sense of self-worth to charge doesn't make it alright for you to do the same. So when you work for free set a strict timescale (probably no more than a month or so) and stick to it. If the magazine, newspaper or website doesn't want to pay you after that time either you aren't good enough or, more likely, they know they can get copy elsewhere without paying. Don't be that guy.

Selling it twice

Your aim is to sell every piece at least twice. Kind of. You sell it once to your primary outlet and then extensively revise it until it is unrecognizable before selling it again to a completely different outlet.

This takes skill, because you cannot – absolutely cannot – sell the same copy twice without upsetting everyone involved and destroying your reputation. But that piece on the evolution of the Porsche 911 over the years could be transformed into a lovely little buyers' guide too. No research is wasted, especially when you can use it twice.

Summary

- Be original in your pitches – and persistent.
- Consider sending a completed piece off to demonstrate ability.
- The only time working for free is worthwhile is to gain experience – and only then for a short, time-bounded period.
- Don't sell yourself cheap, but don't price yourself out of the market either.
- If you can sell it once then you can sell it twice.

Putting it all together

Remember what I said about grammar? I meant it. You're dead in the water if your grammar or spelling is poor. Most copy needs tweaking by someone who didn't write it but if the sub-editor has to re-write the whole piece you can guarantee you'll never be commissioned again. Sub-editors are powerful so you upset them at your peril.

So make sure you're familiar with the publication's house style and make sure you're in line with it; when you're rich and famous you can write whatever you like, however you like and about whatever the hell you like. But not now, not yet. Now is the time to prove to your editor that you're a serious writer who can be trusted with the important stuff like word count, deadline, and style. So get them right.

Before you finally email the polished copy to your editor (or post it on your blog) try looking at it as a PDF, or as a printout, or written in a different font. Your brain tends to read what it *thinks* you've written not what you actually have written, so you need to fool it to check for tempo, clarity, typos, and facts. Sounds dumb, but it works and it's saved me from making a fool of myself more than once.

After you've checked for typos recheck that you've covered everything you thought was important when you made your road test notes. Then look at the editor's brief again. You'll be surprised how often you overlook something important and if you pick it up this early you'll be the only person who knows what an idiot you really are.

Then make sure you've got all the images you are going to need and that they're in the preferred format. I use shared folders on Dropbox but some companies use different systems; if in doubt, ask.

Do you understand the difference between Adobe RGB and sRGB? Between JPEG and TIFF? If not, find out, but for what it's worth, I send everything as high-quality JPEGs, giving them RGB and sRGB: RGB for print and sRGB for websites, sent in different folders that are carefully labelled.

Sleep on it before you double-check it all again. Then get someone else to triple check it. Now, and only now, is it ready to be sent off. Along with your invoice of course.

Summary

- Re-read the editor's brief before you click 'send'.
- Read it as a print out or as a PDF to help you spot the typos and awkward sentences.
- Don't forget the invoice.
- Double-check it again before you press 'send'!

Don't peak too early

It's easy to click 'send' and assume that your work is done. It isn't. One-off commissions have their place and will get you started but becoming a regular contributor is far better – and much harder.

Hone your craft

Seeing your first piece in print, or on a website, is a magical moment, so enjoy it. Open a bottle of something nice and savour the moment. Show it to friends and add it to your online clippings service. Share it across your social media platforms and enjoy the fact that you are now a motoring journalist.

Because the hard work starts now.

You need to compare the published piece with what you actually wrote. If you're good – no, make that very good – the two pieces will be identical. The rest of us get to examine what changes the editor or sub-editor made. Sometimes they'll have done a wonderful job, turning a body of turgid, metaphor-heavy rubbish into something light and frothy and wonderfully readable.

Sometimes they will ruin it.

But that's OK, because you cannot afford to be too precious about your work. It's not *War and Peace,* after all, is it? (Actually, that's not quite true. I did resign from an outlet on principle once after it mangled my work once too often. I'm an idiot, though, as we've seen; don't be like me.)

No, what you are doing here is seeing what the editor actually wanted to publish and using that knowledge to make sure that he or she doesn't have to spend quite so long editing your next piece.

There is going to be a next piece, isn't there?

Snaring your editor

So how to you snare an editor? How do you make it into their Little Black Book of trusted freelancers? The answer is simple, but frustratingly difficult.

You start to build trust by delivering an interesting first piece that is beautifully and accurately written, to the right word count, and delivered (with images) before the deadline. You become invaluable by doing this time after time after time. This is simple.

The difficulties start here

It's easy to come up with one great idea. Hell, even I've done it. The difficulties start in following up the first great pitch with another followed by another – and to keep this going for the coming months and years. OK, you might get lucky by asking them: "is there anything else I can help you with?" but it's unlikely.

Some of your best ideas will come from social media feeds, not the news. So look at what people are talking about and find another angle. As I've said before, you don't have to be first but you do have to be the best, so don't just post the same stock images of a concept car as everyone else, find a unique angle and cover that instead.

Or, why not use Instagram to see what pictures people are liking and commenting on? The chances are that if they like a heavily filtered shot of a Jaguar E-type enough to click on it – and I do accept that clicking on a heart symbol is just about the lowest form of social media engagement it is possible to imagine – they would probably like to see a short, photo-heavy feature on the same car.

Write the headlines first

For fast-moving stories you need to capture your readers' attention and you do this with a headline. So write ten headlines for every story. Then pick your favourite and use that in big, bold type in your pitch.

Editors know better than anyone that it's headlines that lure readers in, and a good headline can make the difference between a thousand people reading your story or a million. (But if you ever use clickbait expressions like: 'you won't believe what happens next' I will hunt you down.)

Summary

- Review every piece of published work to see how you could have written it better. If your editor has changed your work, make sure you understand why they did what they did.
- Social media is a rich source of ideas.
- Headlines matter almost as much as content.

Conclusion

To make the grade as a full-time motoring journalist you'll need to be persistent and develop the skin of a rhino. It will probably take years to get established and you'll be knocked down more times than you can possibly imagine by people who will tell you that it can't be done.

But it can and when you're out driving in the sun with the roof down, or talking nonsense with your colleagues in a bar halfway across the world, or writing in the small hours there is no better job in the world.

It just doesn't pay very much. OK?

All photographs and images are © Carlton Boyce unless otherwise indicated.

Printed in Great Britain
by Amazon